renoir

renoir

Text by
PAMELA PRITZKER

LEON AMIEL • PUBLISHER
NEW YORK

Published by
LEON AMIEL • PUBLISHER
NEW YORK
ISBN 0-8148-0663-5
Printed in the United States of America

Pierre Auguste Renoir was born on February 25, 1841, in Limoges, France. In 1845, his father, a tailor by trade, moved the family to Paris with hopes of finding his fortune in the capital. They moved into a small apartment which had been part of a sixteenth century housing complex for the Palace Guard. They were situated at the end of the Tuileries Palace and young Renoir and his friends played in the courtyard of the Louvre. He developed, throughout his childhood, an intense love of the city, its streets and its people. This would later be translated into vivid and colorful Impressionist paintings of Parisian street life.

Renoir was not an exceptional student. Perhaps this was due to his generally shy and quiet personality. He had a terrible fear of drawing any attention to himself and retained this dislike throughout his career. Yet, his kindness and good nature won him many life-long friendships. Although Renoir had three other brothers, he always felt much closer to his mother and his sister, Lisa. This special affinity towards women shines forth in all his later paintings, especially his sensually glowing and voluptuous nudes.

As a child, Renoir was constantly doodling in his schoolbooks or drawing with a piece of chalk on the floors at home. He would quickly sketch anyone in sight. Unlike many other families in the mid-nineteenth century, his did not consider drawing a worthless pursuit, rather, they respected it as an honorable craft. This attitude was instilled within Renoir to such a degree that he later described himself, not as an artist, but as a "workman-painter." During this same period, young Renoir joined the choir at the Church of St. Eustache. The then unknown choir-master, Charles Gounod, found Renoir to have a promising voice and offered him free lessons and the inducement of a future as an exceedingly well-paid opera star. Renoir had now come of age to be apprenticed into a career. However, he was also offered an apprenticeship with a porcelain factory. The choice which lay before Renoir was left to fate. He would later speak of it in his theory of the cork floating with the tide. Thus, he followed his father's natural preference for the craft which Limoges, their hometown, was famous for, and Renoir began his career as a decorator and painter of earthenware in the works of M. Levy. By 1854, Renoir was industriously painting 18th century profiles of Marie Antoinette by the dozens and gradually began to vary the theme with 18th century styled nudes. Throughout this job, Laporte, a painter friend of Renoir's, urged him to copy the Old Masters in the Louvre. However, he had absolutely no thoughts of becoming a professional painter at this time. He was earning a sufficient salary and was enjoying his life; two principles which were to be his guiding lights all his life. However, he did accept lessons in life-drawing and oil painting from an old china decorator he met at the works. Soon, he developed a great love for the works of Delacroix and the 18th century painters of sensual nudes which he discovered at the Louvre. His love for the sensual began to manifest itself in an overwhelming love of women. He found them rotund and voluptuous, soft to touch, yet with an underlying strength, which his later nudes universally expressed.

During the five years at the works, Renoir began long explorations on foot throughout Paris. On one of these jaunts, he discovered the

16th century Fontaine des Innocents. He sat down and began to sketch the bas-reliefs as potential porcelain designs. However, he became "spellbound" by the figures of women, specifically those sculpted by Jean Goujon. He wondered why Goujon's figures were so much more exciting than the others. This difference enthralled him. Later he was to remark, "Goujon gives you the texture of flesh and knows how to make drapery cling to the figure. Until then I hadn't realized how drapery brings out the form." This revelation changed Renoir's concept of Art, with a capital "A", to art, with a small, personal "a". Throughout his long life, Renoir would return to the Fontaine to learn from Goujon. In his last years of life, no longer capable of walking, he advised his son, Jean, the film director, to give it another look.

At the age of sixteen, Renoir unveiled his first oil painting. This critical moment met with praise from Laporte, his family and the old porcelain decorator. However, it would be some time before Renoir would consider himself an artist. He continued to paint porcelain until automation rendered hand decorated porcelain obsolete. M. Levy was forced to close down the workshop, and Renoir found work decorating fans. Because the fans required different subject matter and themes than the earthenware, Renoir renewed his visits to the Louvre in search of workable ideas. He discovered the sensuous, if sometimes frivolous, works of Fragonard, Boucher and Watteau. His taste in art was being formed. As he later stated about Boucher's "Diane au bain": "(it) was the first picture to thrill me, and I've continued to love it all my life as one does love one's first loves."

In the 1850's, to supplement his income, Renoir painted some twenty murals for various cafes. These, unfortunately, were strictly freelance, but he finally found a steadier income painting blinds, for missionaries in the Far East. Although he managed to save a large amount of money while painting the blinds, he was unbearably bored with the task. Becoming unhappy with his work was a major violation of the third principle of his life code. So, for the first time in his young life, Renoir began to seriously consider his friends' urging him to become a serious painter.

In the spring of 1862, after much consideration by the family and the pleadings of Laporte, Renoir arrived at Gleyre's studio, an affiliate of the Ecole des Beaux-Arts.

At this point, 19th century French art was divided into two very distinct categories. There was "good" art which was accepted by the Academy and shown each year at the official exhibition. These works were in the tradition of David and Ingres, or dealt with military scenes, considered to be suitably dignified for painters to represent. The opponents of this style were inspired by the works of Delacroix, who had abandoned dark pigments and neo-classical subject matter. Those artists who were to follow the teachings of Delacroix were soon to find themselves poverty striken outcasts from the art market.

Before entering Gleyre's studio, Renoir had already become an avid admirer of Delacroix's paintings in the Louvre. However, in his first few weeks at the studio, he not only discovered that very few students were indeed seriously pursuing careers as artists, but also that his preference for Delacroix would be a handicap. He showed one of his early oils to Signol, who had been lecturing in the evening at the Beaux-Arts. Signol's reply to Renoir was a warning to be careful that he didn't "become a second Delacroix."

Thus, from the very first, Renoir had two counts against him at Gleyre's: he was a serious student, and he preferred the rebellious style of Delacroix. He also realized that he would have to learn on his own and began spending nights at the studio working out visual problems on canvas. This separated him from all the other students, except one, Alfred Sisley. They became close friends and worked together towards developing a style which they could honestly embrace. They held different opinions on art; Sisley preferred Corot, while Renoir felt more akin to the dramatic landscapes of Diaz. This led to many robust discussions at the neighborhood cafe, Closerie des Lilas.

In 1863, Frederic Bazille joined the studio. He was in a much better financial situation than Renoir. He was also much more sociable and was always ready to go out on the town or to a chic party. At the same time, another student, Claude Monet, joined the little group. Monet, like Renoir, immediately came into conflict with Gleyre for painting his model too realistically. According to Gleyre, this was "very ugly" to look at.

Although Monet had very little money to support himself with, he dressed each and every day as if he were going to a fancy dress ball. Together, they presented quite a contrast, Renoir in his overalls and Monet in his silk suits. It was Bazille who eventually brought the two together and completed the group of rebels who were to become the leaders of the Impressionist school of painting.

As the year went on, Monet became active against what the other three felt was reactionary at the Beaux-Arts. He urged them to quit and join the open-air painters in the country. A compromise was finally reached. They agreed to a painting sojourn out-of-doors, if Monet would accompany them to the Louvre and study the Old Masters.

Soon, Renoir and Bazille were sharing living and studio quarters in Paris. Bazille introduced him to many wealthy patrons of the arts and the avant-garde of the cultural revolution, including Baudelaire and Manet. Bazille brought him along to the "in" salons of the day and Renoir became welcomed as an unaffected guest with refreshingly honest opinions. During this period Bazille was constantly bringing "new talent" to their studio. Two of these novices were Camille Pissarro and Paul Cezanne. Renoir felt very close to Pissarro, who was of a similar family background and equally knowledgeable of painting. Cezanne, although of a wealthy family, had refused their help, despising anything middle class. He was extremely honest and, like Renoir, spoke his exact feelings, in plain and simple language. However, more important than all of this, Cezanne shared Renoir's intense admiration for Delacroix's passionate colors.

By Easter of 1863, Renoir was beginning to have doubts about his success as a painter. His savings were dwindling and the few sales he made were to charitable patrons. Yet, he went for an outdoor painting sojourn with Monet over the Easter holidays. Monet considered the contemporary Barbizon school of landscape painters unexciting, because they only sketched and made studies out-of-doors. They reserved the actual painting for the studio. The small group of rebels sought lodgings at the Cheval Blanc Inn, and they immediately began to *paint* outside. Renoir found that he enjoyed painting in the open-air because it allowed him to work quickly, with a minimum of advance preparation. He did not abide by Monet's theories but painted solely for pleasure. As he later stated: "For me, a picture should be a pleasant thing, joyful and pretty—yes pretty!" His life's work illustrates truth of this saying.

The following year saw the closing of Gleyre's studio. Renoir returned to the Cheval Blanc Inn to paint out-of-doors with Sisley. Two major events occurred while he was in the country. First, he had a chance of meeting with Diaz, the landscape artist he so greatly admired. He persuaded Diaz to look at a half-finished canvas. Diaz remarked that the drawing was not bad (greatly to the surprise of Renoir, who felt his drawing was inadequate), but he criticized Renoir's using too much black pigment. From this point on, Renoir threw away bitumen and thoroughly embraced the glorious bright colors he had always loved.

The second event, which also caused a change in Renoir, was the acceptance of his painting "La Esmeralda" by the Salon jury. It was quite unusual for an unknown, twenty-three year old painter to have his first painting accepted by the Academy. However, when he returned to Paris he destroyed the painting, which was dark and colorless due to an excessive use of bitumen.

The next year was spent preparing for the 1865 Salon. Renoir was luckier than the year before and had several commissioned portraits from which he could support himself. Once again his painting was accepted, and he returned to Chailly to paint with his friends. Monet's work had also been accepted by the Salon, and with renewed confidence he began to expect Sisley and Renoir to serve as his male models. This forced the two to move from Chailly to Marlotte in search for more free time to paint. Bazille remained with Monet and served as his model.

At Marlotte, they made their home at Mere Anthony's Inn. This move was to prove of monumental importance in the next several years. In 1866, Renoir met the greatest revolutionary painter of the time, Courbet. His influence can be seen in Renoir's now famous painting of "Mere Anthony's." Here the brushstrokes are stronger in accent and broader on the canvas.

Upon his return to Paris he began to paint street scenes side-by-side with Monet, who was beginning to explore the future colors of Impressionism. Renoir's entry for the Salon was a voluptuous nude which was summarily rejected as being "improper." Undaunted, Renoir added a dead deer and renamed the painting "Diana." Although it was still rejected, he received an offer for the painting; but as Renoir recalled later, ". . . we couldn't come to terms because he wanted to buy the doe only."

The next several years in Paris brought about many changes. This period marked the first discussions of an alternate exhibition, separate from the official salon. Although nothing came of it in 1867, the discussions marked a new outlook. The group from Gleyre's studio sought desperately to find new outlets through which they could sell their works. With the exception of Bazille, they were all terribly poor. It was through the generosity of Bazille that Monet and Renoir survived those long, lean years. Soon, Bazille and Renoir moved to the Batignolles section of Paris, close to the Cafe Guerbois, where Manet was often to be found. The debates were often fierce, and went on late into the night.

This was an extremely exciting period for Renoir. His salon entry had earned him a favorable review by Zacharie Astruc who greatly admired "Lisa a l'ombrelle." He wrote of the grace and delicacy of the figure "in which the whole charm rests in the use of light." Not only did this cheer Renoir in mind and in pocket, but it became a prophecy of the style he would articulate in his future works.

The following spring, Renoir left Paris for Ville d'Avray, the country home his parents had retired to. Several miles down the river, he discovered Ilse de Choissy, on which Pere Fournaise floated a barge/restaurant. There one could drink and enjoy a leisurely lunch on the river. Next to it Fournaise built a wharf on which he placed a dance floor. La Grenouillere became a Garden of Eden to week-ending Parisians. One could dance, eat, drink, swim, go boating: everything one would desire on a summer holiday. It was frequented by all types of people: prostitutes with their pimps taking the day off, young lovers, writers (including Guy de Maupassant) and artists of every sort. Patron Fournaise encouraged all artists to drink with him and would accept a painting in return for a meal. For Renoir, this great conglomerate of people provided a remarkable visual and emotional atmosphere inspiring some of his most enchanting and famous works. One, in particular, was a charming portrait of Mere and Pere Fournaise wearing their aprons and drinking absinthe. At the time this painting was considered ugly and vulgar; however, in his later years of success, Renoir reported that the portrait had miraculously become "noble and dignified." The many summers spent at La

Grenouillere would be of Renoir's happiest. The simple pleasures of painting people whom he loved, of being surrounded by artists and artisans, of having a good night of drinking and dancing with robust women—these were the loves of Renoir's life and shine forth in his glorious paintings of La Grenouillere.

Upon returning to Paris, the pleasure of the summer quickly faded. Monet was destitute. The only painting to be accepted in the salon was Renoir's gypsy study, which he had painted the past summer at Ville d'Avray. Out of dismay Renoir suggested that Monet settle outside of Paris in order to live more cheaply. Thus, by the next summer, Monet and Renoir were neighbors in the country.

Initially, Renoir stayed at his home in Ville d'Avray, often visiting the Monets at Bougival, near La Grenouillere. One day Renoir saw a canvas which Monet was working on. It was unlike any other Renoir had ever seen. It was a composite of small brush strokes of pure color, without a drop of black. The figures and background simply vibrated with light. Renoir sat down and began to paint the same scene. Differences appeared in the two canvasses and in those that were to follow. Renoir began to explore the technique of what would soon be known as Impressionism. However, unlike Monet, whose main interest lay in the purity of landscape, Renoir continued to explore the human figure, particularly that of robust young women.

"La Grenouillere" which Renoir painted at this time, is radiant with warm and glowing colors, creating a new visual reality of joyous feeling. And yet, all was not well with Renoir. Like the others, he had no money, no patron, and no chance of selling his works. He kept on painting and finally received a commission from the wealthy Charpentier brothers. In addition, two more works were accepted by the Salon, yet none were to be sold.

In 1870, when the Franco-Prussian War broke out, the original group was completely broken up. Cezanne left for L'Estaque, in Southern France; Monet, Sisley and Pissarro left for England leaving in Paris only Renoir and Bazille. Renoir decided to leave himself open to fate. He was drafted into a cavalry division, and saw no action throughout the war. Bazille, on the other hand, joined the Zoaves in order to be in the heart of the fight. Four months later, to the great sorrow and despair of Renoir, he was killed.

Upon Renoir's return to Paris, the political atmosphere of the Commune was absolute chaos. Yet, Renoir had friends on both sides and managed to travel back and forth from Ville d'Avray to Paris with a minimum of danger.

As Paris began to recover from the war, Renoir's friends began their return. The group was once more together with Monet taking the role as leader. He and Renoir picked up their painting where they had left off: at the threshold of Impressionism. The search for a new visual perception of reality was almost over, yet just beginning. They perceived color as changes in light in an overall effect, not just in small, localized areas. However, these realizations were not immediate, and Renoir's own progress was not steady-paced.

His paintings in the early 1870's vary greatly in style and technique. The influence of Manet, can be seen in the harshly clashing colors of "Portrait of Madame Maitre" (1870). In 1872, Renoir modelled his "Parisian Women Dressed as Algerians" after his beloved Delacroix's "Women of Algiers." Although these were far from his best efforts, we can see Renoir's preoccupation with texture and color. This overriding preference for sculptured forms and smooth textures would eventually cause him to stray from the basic concepts of Impressionism.

With the return to normalcy in France, Renoir began once more to paint out-of-doors. It is within these early landscapes, rather than in his portraits, that we see the full bloom of Impressionism. In the "Pont-Neuf" we find the vibrating atmosphere and sunlight bordering of luminosity which was to become Renoir's trademark. In 1873, Renoir and Monet both set out for the country to paint side-by-side, as they had done in the years before the war. Although they painted the same scenes, (see "Pont Neuf," "Sailboats at Argenteuil") Renoir's work tended to be lighter and freer in spirit. In the "Pont Neuf" the difference between the two painters is most obvious. Renoir chose a sunlit, gleaming day, full of brightly colored parasols. On the other hand, Monet's depiction is dark and gloomy, painted on a rainy day with an enveloping moody atmosphere.

These years, 1872-1883, mark the Impressionist period for Renoir. Although his paintings were infinitely more joyous and celebrative in nature than Monet's it was Monet who returned to France with confidence in a brighter future. While in England, Monet, Pissarro and Sisley met the art dealer, Paul Durand-Ruel who had been a consistent buyer of Barbizon paintings. He immediately bought up their works and produced exhibitions in London. Thus, for the first time, the tiny group of artists had an enthusiastic art dealer behind them. Renoir remarked, "In 1873 an event took place in my life: I made the acquaintance of Durand-Ruel, the first picture-dealer, the only one for many long years, to have faith in me." However, Durand-Ruel's ability to attract buyers declined.

He suffered great financial difficulties and was forced for the time being to abandon the Impressionists.

Renoir was forced to move from his old studio, for lack of rent. He relocated far from his creditors, across the Seine to Montmartre, which was still a small village, not yet incorporated into the city of Paris. His new studio became the hub of artistic discussion for the Impressionists. He became engrossed in his work and created a daily routine which he would follow all the years he lived there.

In 1874, once again the question arose of how to market their paintings. However, this time, the idea of a separate exhibition by the group of outcasts from the Salon seemed to be the answer. They felt the time was ripe for public and critical acceptance. Durand-Ruel prepared a catalogue with an introduction by Sylvestre, a supporter of the group. He claimed that far from being revolutionary painters, these young men were simply the inheritors of the tradition of Delacroix, Courbet, Millet and Corot. The catalogue was the first literary attempt at legitimizing the school of Impressionists.

On April 15, 1874, the first group show took place in the photographic studios of Nadar. The exhibition included works by Monet, Renoir, Sisley, Boudin, Pissarro, Degas, Cezanne and Berthe Morisot. However, much to their disappointment, neither the critics nor the public were ready to accept the works. In fact, out of all the reviews, which were extremely derogatory, Renoir's eight entries fared out the best. However, this was certainly not the success they had hoped for and aside from the publicity caused by the scandalized critics, the group experienced little change in their financial situation. The only positive effect of the exhibit was the dubbing of the group, "Impressionist," by an exceedingly outraged critic who was ridiculing Monet's work entitled, "Impression, Sunrise."

As a result of the disastrous exhibition they decided against another showing the following year. However, since they still desperately needed to sell their works, Renoir suggested that they hold an auction. He felt that this would accomplish two things: first, it would raise enough money to pay back the costs of the previous year's exhibition; second, it would enable them to plan a second exhibition the following year.

In March, 1875, Monet, Renoir, Sisley and Berthe Morisot arranged for an auction to be held at the Hotel Drouot. Unfortunately, the auction proved to be more of a failure than the exhibition. The Parisian art world was scandalized and felt that these young artists must surely be making fun of the public. Durand-Ruel suggested that they each buy back their works, thus thrusting themselves back into even greater poverty.

For Renoir, the auction provided one happy event. He met Chocquet, a minor official in the customs bureau. At this time, it certainly was not necessary to be wealthy in order to collect art. M. Chocquet, began to buy Renoir's works and commissioned him to paint the "Portrait of Madame Chocquet." It was M. Chocquet's generosity and kind-heartedness that kept Renoir's spirits going immediately after the crushing fiasco of the auction.

The following months brought several commissions from other patrons who had witnessed the auction. One, in particular, for M. Clapisson, was a group portrait of his family, for which he offered Renoir the astounding sum of twelve hundred francs. Following this generous offer Renoir moved his living quarters to the heart of Montmartre keeping his studio on Rue St.-Georges. He once again enjoyed the pleasures which Montmartre had to offer and began to paint and sketch street scenes. He frequented the Moulin de la Galette, a large, open air dance hall and cafe which was the center of activity for the young people of Montmartre. Renoir fell in love with the atmosphere and color of the Moulin and began to sketch the activities while on the premises. He convinced his friends to pose as dancers with local girls as their partners. The final painting, entitled, "Le Moulin de la Galette," was finished in 1876. Renoir captured Paris of the 1870's as a gay and joyous city, full of beautiful young girls, in gaily colored dresses, dancing their hearts away. He combined his preference for bright color with lighting diffused throughout in patches of sun and shadow. This masterpiece is perhaps the complete statement of Renoir's love affair with life.

The rest of the year was spent in a torrent of work. Renoir painted a variety of subjects, including portraits, a study of a young girl in a theatre box ("La Premiere Sortie"), group compositions, and an extremely beautiful arrangement of flowers. Of the "Bouquet devant la glace" Renoir explained: "I give my brain a rest by painting flowers. . . . When I paint flowers I sometimes experiment, I play about with values fearlessly, without the dread of ruining a canvas." Perhaps it is due to this fearless experimenting that the painting is an absolute delight of color and light.

The artists began to plan a third exhibition. This time it was held at Durand-Ruel's gallery and was by far the most representative of all the shows. Once again the critics' response was heartbreaking. However, Renoir's contributions were the best works he had done to date. They included "Le Moulin de la Galette," commissioned portraits of the Charpentier family and portraits of the actress Jeanne Samary, whom Renoir described as "a ray of sunshine."

Although for the third time the critics voiced their outrage, the Impressionists were making a name for themselves and becoming well known to the public. However, they sold only one or two works and their morale was definitely falling. Following the exhibition, on Renoir's suggestion, they held another auction. Unlike the first, this one was held in the utmost seriousness and the bidding prices were a bit higher.

The next year, Renoir found a new buyer for his works, Eugene Murer. Throughout the years, Murer bought up many of the Impressionists' works at a fraction of their real worth. However, he kept Renoir in enough money to be able to continue to paint and to maintain his studio. As the spring approached, discussion began on the fourth Impressionist exhibition. Renoir made his decision against participating in favor of entering the 1878 Salon. This created a schism between Renoir and the others who had decided against participation in both. For Renoir, this simply cleared the air of any doubts he may have had, and he, Cezanne and Manet all submitted their works. Cezanne's and Manet's works were rejected. Renoir's painting, entitled, "Marguerite" or "La tasse de chocolat" was accepted. It was the type of painting the Salon jury and the audience would find appealing. It was brightly painted with the usual sense of well-being found in all of Renoir's work.

The success of "La tasse de chocolat" brought Renoir another commission from the Charpentiers and he was already planning for the following year's Salon entry. Although the rest of the year was harsh on his fellow painters, they looked forward with renewed hope to the 1879 Impressionist Exhibition. Much to their surprise, the exhibition was a success, financially and critically. For the first time each exhibitor showed a profit. The reviewers had lost their animosity towards the style they had so ruefully entitled Impressionism.

Renoir submitted his group portrait of the Charpentier family to the 1879 Salon. Not only was it accepted, but it was hung low enough to be seen and with enough light to be appreciated. Due to Mme. Charpentier's insistence and influence over the jury, Renoir experienced a measure of success.

Through the Charpentier family Renoir met another wealthy patron, Paul Berard. They immediately became best of friends and Berard invited Renoir to the Chateau de Wargemont, near Dieppe, to do a portrait of his daughter. This was to be the first of many enjoyable and profitable visits with Berard. Throughout the summer he painted Berard's family and eventually painted "Les rosiers de Wargemont." This study of Berard's rose garden was described by Van Gogh as "Renoir's magnificent rose garden."

Upon his return to Paris, Renoir began to prepare for the next Salon. Monet joined him and together they decided to seek new markets for their works. This created another split in the ranks of the Impressionists. Renoir and Monet no longer felt that the group had maintained its artistic integrity and standards. Their works were accepted by the jury, but without the patronage of Mme. Charpentier, their paintings were hung almost out of sight.

Not to be dissuaded by this turn of events, Renoir arranged for a one-man show of Monet's work at the offices of *Vie Moderne* (a contemporary art journal). The response was so overwhelmingly favorable, that Duret claimed that Monet was "the only original landscape artist since Corot." After many, many years of abject poverty and critical disappointment, Monet, too, had finally attained recognition.

At a time when Renoir should have been content with success after years of struggle, he only seemed to become more dissatisfied. He felt that at his age, which was forty, he should have settled into a style. Yet, he was not happy with his painting, and as a result he returned to Mere Fournaise in an attempt to sort out his feelings about his work. He decided at the end of the summer to change studios and search for a large commission in order to pay for a journey to Algeria. At the same time, Durand-Ruel began to get back on his feet as a dealer and buy up as many Impressionist works as possible in an effort to gain a monopoly. Renoir did not sell to Durand-Ruel whom he feared would, by monopolizing the market, ultimately lower the sale price. With his work in a competitive market and money in his pocket from a commissioned portrait of Cahen d'Anvers' daughter, Renoir left for Algeria.

Although artistically the trip to Algeria was not very productive, Renoir returned from the trip feeling much more at ease with himself. At the age of forty, Renoir decided that it was almost time for him to settle down. Throughout the long struggle, Renoir had never allowed himself to become too involved with a woman, although his great affection for women was well known. When Renoir met his future wife, Aline Charigot, she was only fourteen, twenty-one years younger than himself. They would meet in the local *cremerie* where Renoir took his daily lunches. During this time, there was never any serious discussion of marriage, yet, a very strong friendship developed. She posed for "La Tonnelle" and for "Sortie du Conservatoire" at the age of fifteen. When Renoir returned from Algeria, Aline was nineteen and of marriageable age. However, she could feel Renoir's hesitancy and postponed any plans for marriage until he returned from his long awaited sojourn in Italy.

Before he departed, he, Aline and many of his old friends left Paris for a summer of painting at La Grenouillere. The summer of 1881 was a wonderfully exciting time for Renoir. He was in love and surrounded by all the people and places he loved. His exuberance for life shines forth in his third masterpiece, "Le dejeuner des canotiers," in the tradition of "Le Moulin de la Galette" and "La Grenouillere." This painting shows all of his friends on the balcony of La Grenouillere partaking in a typical French lunch. Their gaiety and joy is overflowing. Aline sits in the foreground of the picture holding a little dog in her lap. It is the mystique of the face with which we have become so familiar in Renoir's portraits. Through his love for Aline, we have come to know her better than any other painter's wife in the history of Modern Art.

Soon, Renoir decided to leave his friends and

Aline for a last soul searching journey. Abruptly he departed into Italy to observe first-hand the works of Raphael and the haunting sun-lit canals of Venice. He was in search of a true style to which he could adhere. Although his sketches and paintings of Italy are not exceptional, they gave him the opportunity to experiment with color and technique. It is interesting to note that while he was on his way home, he received a commission to paint Wagner's portrait at his villa in Palermo. Wagner would only agree to a half-hour sitting. When Renoir was hastily finished, Wagner asked to see the portrait. He commented that Renoir had made him look like a "Protestant minister." Fortunately, Renoir eventually sold the portrait in Paris.

Travelling north to Paris, Renoir stopped at L'Estaque to visit with Cezanne. He began to paint out-of-doors in the brilliant sunlight of southern France simplifying the details of his paintings and striving for a true expression of his feelings. However, the weather took a sudden change and Renoir's health deteriorated rapidly into pneumonia. At this time in Paris the seventh Impressionist show was being organized by Durand-Ruel. Although Renoir refused to contribute to the show, Durand-Ruel exhibited the works which were already in his possession. This show was the least representative of all the exhibitions and trumpeted the demise of Impressionism as a group.

Renoir returned to Paris, with his thoughts completely on Aline. They were soon married and following a honeymoon in Sicily, they took up residence in Renoir's Montmarte studio. Although he found happiness in Aline, his discontentment with his own work increased. He no longer believed in his abilities as an artist. For the next three years he was to struggle with his work and concentrate on what he believed to be his main weakness: drawing. He returned to the study of Old Masters in the Louvre and began to consciously improve his studies of human figure. His paintings during this period were harsh and linear without any of the sensual tones of his earlier works.

In the summer of 1883, Renoir went to the island of Guernsey for a painting holiday. Like many of his previous painting trips this was not exceptionally productive. However, he did enjoy himself tremendously and two months later set off with Monet to southern France in order to visit Cezanne. Yet, they did not paint together as they had done so often in the past.

Upon his return to Paris, Renoir found his commissions dwindling. Durand-Ruel's major source of income, the Union Centrale, was heading towards bankruptcy, and only one of

Renoir's paintings was accepted by the Salon. This would be the last time any of his paintings would be accepted for the next seven years. For the next several years he would seek out new haunts and make numerous journeys outside of Paris in an effort to pull himself out of the harsh, linear style he was experimenting with.

By 1885 Renoir had recovered from his painting slump to discover the artistic expression now considered to be the style of the mature Renoir. He had found a new retreat, La Roche-Guyon, and it was here that he began to see and feel a new sensibility towards his paintings. As he wrote to Durand-Ruel: "I think I shall give you pleasure this time. I have recovered, never to leave it, the old painting, sweet and light. . . ." However, this was only the beginning of Renoir's struggle. It would last another ten long years.

During these years, Renoir's art work was of a very stiff and lifeless nature. He was seeking the secret behind the masterpieces of Ingres. whose works he would copy for hours in the Louvre. Ironically, for the first time the Impressionists were accepted as a legitimate school of art, yet Renoir rejected their tradition and went back to the eighteenth century masters for his teachers. This new style brought him much criticism and very few commissions. Throughout this period, Renoir travelled extensively in France and

Europe. He found that he could not concentrate in one place for longer than several months at a time. It was also at this time, that Renoir suffered his first attack of rheumatism, which would become a crippling disease within fifteen years. Often, he sought the warmth of Southern France, in particular the Midi, where he finally settled in his old age.

In 1895, Renoir attained the freedom of style which he had sought for so many long and arduous years. This first year was heralded with a charming portrait of his son Jean and the other members of his family. In this painting which is entitled "La famille de l'artiste" Renoir seems to have tossed overboard all the restraints of the previous ten years. The colors are gay, the mood joyful and serene. The harsh outlining found in all his *maniere aigre* works is softened and he exploits the pigment to attain a smooth surface.

Over the next year, each canvas became increasingly freer from stiffness and immobility. He did numerous child studies during this period, each with a new sense of vivid reality and celebration of life. His technique reflected the many years spent in perfecting drawing and experimenting with exquisite color combinations.

His family by this time had been augmented by two women, who were to serve as models for Renoir's finest nude studies. Gabrielle was employed as a nanny for little Jean, and La Boulangere as a servant. Both were fine, robust models, who maintained their provincial honesty and beauty. Renoir's paintings of these two women attracted Parisian art dealer, Vollard. Although he would never become as important a dealer for Renoir as Durand-Ruel, a strong friendship developed which led to Vollard's two highly informative books on Renoir and his art. In them, Vollard related many of Renoir's personal habits and idiosyncracies, but most of all he imparts Renoir's youthful and enthusiastic love for painting and living, which were one and the same to Renoir. A remark was once made which perfectly described Renoir, "Painting a woman excites him more than going to bed with her."

The next several years were marked by increasing financial success. There were numerous one-man shows and finally an entire room at the Salon d'Autome was reserved for his works. In 1904, at age sixty-three Renoir was being hailed as one of the greatest living French artists.

Unfortunately, his health declined. He bought a new house in Essoyes, where his wife had once lived. One day while bicycling in rainy weather he fell and broke his arm. Although the arm was set, the bone would never heal properly, and shortly after the cast was off he discovered that his arm was stricken by arthritis.

Nevertheless, Renoir continued to paint glorious works. He pursued cures for the rheumatism and arthritis at numerous spas, knowing all the while that there was no cure. By 1903, Renoir had moved to Cagnes, in Southern France where he hoped that the warmth and sun would allow him to paint with a minimum of pain.

He spent the winters at Cagnes painting as well as he could. The rheumatism was crippling his body and the arthritis crippling his hands. Yet, he continued to paint the beautiful in life, not the ugly. His morale could not have been good, for over the next few years he was to outlive many of the friends and artists he had loved dearly.

By 1908, Renoir had moved into a new period of painting, his red period. He could not paint a red vibrant enough. Each work resounded with red, a color which represented the full blossoming of life. Life was painting for Renoir; perhaps his love affair with red was the last chance he had to enjoy life's wonders.

In 1912, he suffered the most severe bout yet with rheumatism. It left his arms and legs paralyzed. The next year he was operated on and regained partial use of his arms, but for the rest of his life he would be bound to a wheelchair. Even these hardships could not dissuade Renoir from painting. He looked on the positive side and remarked, "Now I'll *have* to paint all the time." He maintained his delightful sense of humor and continued to charm his many sympathetic visitors.

At the age of seventy-five, Renoir could no longer hold a brush. He continued to paint and sketch with the brush strapped to his hand and the pallet on his lap. In the midst of all this despair a new model, Andree was introduced to him. He painted this young sixteen year old girl in the most delightful poses. For Renoir, Andree's wonderful skin tones were better than any curative. He began to paint at an astonishing rate, creating bathing scenes and nudes as if he were a man of twenty.

This renewal of life lasted until 1919. Just before his death, he was invited to view the Louvre in a private opening. There he saw many of his own works and those other artists' with whom he had struggled. This last bit of irony, to be so honored by the state and to even have his paintings properly hung, when for so many years his works were not even accepted by the Salon, was certainly not lost on Renoir. Upon his return to Cagnes, he continued to paint with even more fervor, perhaps knowing that time was no longer a friend. In November, he caught pneumonia and was never to recover. The man who had insisted on painting only what would bring joy and an indefinable happiness to those who viewed his works would paint no more.

PLATES

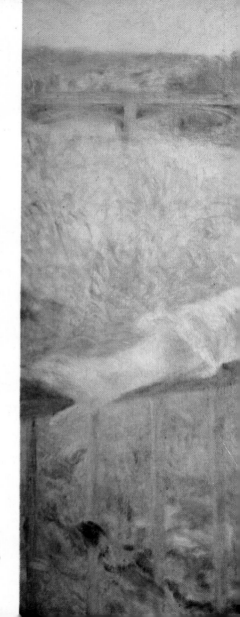

1
Alphonsine Fournaise on the Isle of Chatou
1879

2
Cliffs
1883

3
At the seashore
1875-77

4
Mother and child taking a walk
1874

5
Mesdemoiselles Cahen d'Anvers
1881

6
Road climbing through the fields
1875

8
Moss roses
c. 1880

9　The end of luncheon　1879

10   The loge   1874

11
Confidences
1878

12
Portrait of a model
1878-1880

13
Torso of a woman in sunlight
1876

14
The swing
1876

Girl with a blue and red striped corsage
1875

16
The Moulin de la Galette
1876

17-18   The moulin de la galette (detail)   1876

19
Dance in the city
1883

20
Dance in the country
1883

21
Boating party at Chatou
1879

Girl with auburn hair

23
Brown-haired girl

24
Arabian holiday in Algiers
1881

Girl in a hat with a red feather

26
Mademoiselle Grimpel with a red ribbon
1880

27
Girl on a blue background
1882

28
Mademoiselle Julie Manet
1887

29
Girl: Nini Lopez

30
Girl reading
1892-1895

32
L'Estaque

33
Madame Charpentier and her children
1878

34
Luncheon of the boating party (detail)
1881

35
Luncheon of the boating party
1881

36
Girls cutting flowers
1889

37
Two girls in a meadow
c. 1895

38
Young girls at the piano (preliminary study)

39
Young girls at the piano
1892

40
Two sisters or two little girls
c. 1890

41
Two sisters drawing
1890

43   Little girl in a blue hat   1881

44
Seated nude
c. 1885

45
Nude seated in a landscape
1883

46
Blond bather
1881

47
Bather standing in the water
1888

48-49 Study for "The bathers" 1884-1885

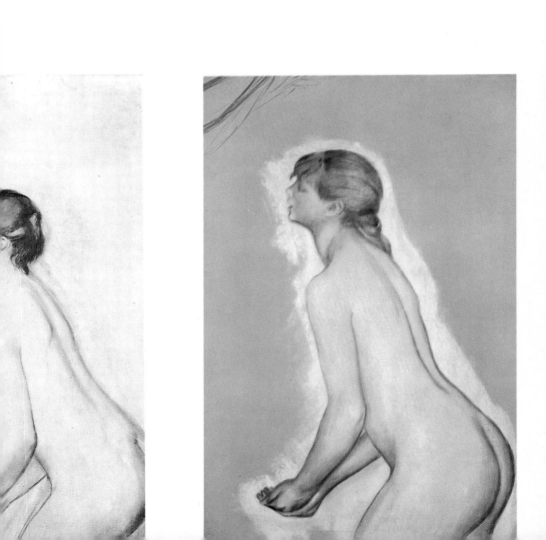

50
The bathers
1887

51
Girl reading (preliminary study)
1890

52
Girl reading
1892-1895

53
Little girl with a hat
1890

54
Berthe Morisot and her daughter

55
Woman with a rose

57
Nude in an armchair
1895-1900

58
Woman sleeping
1897

59   Woman sleeping   1880

60   Woman sleeping (detail)   1897

61
House in Cagnes

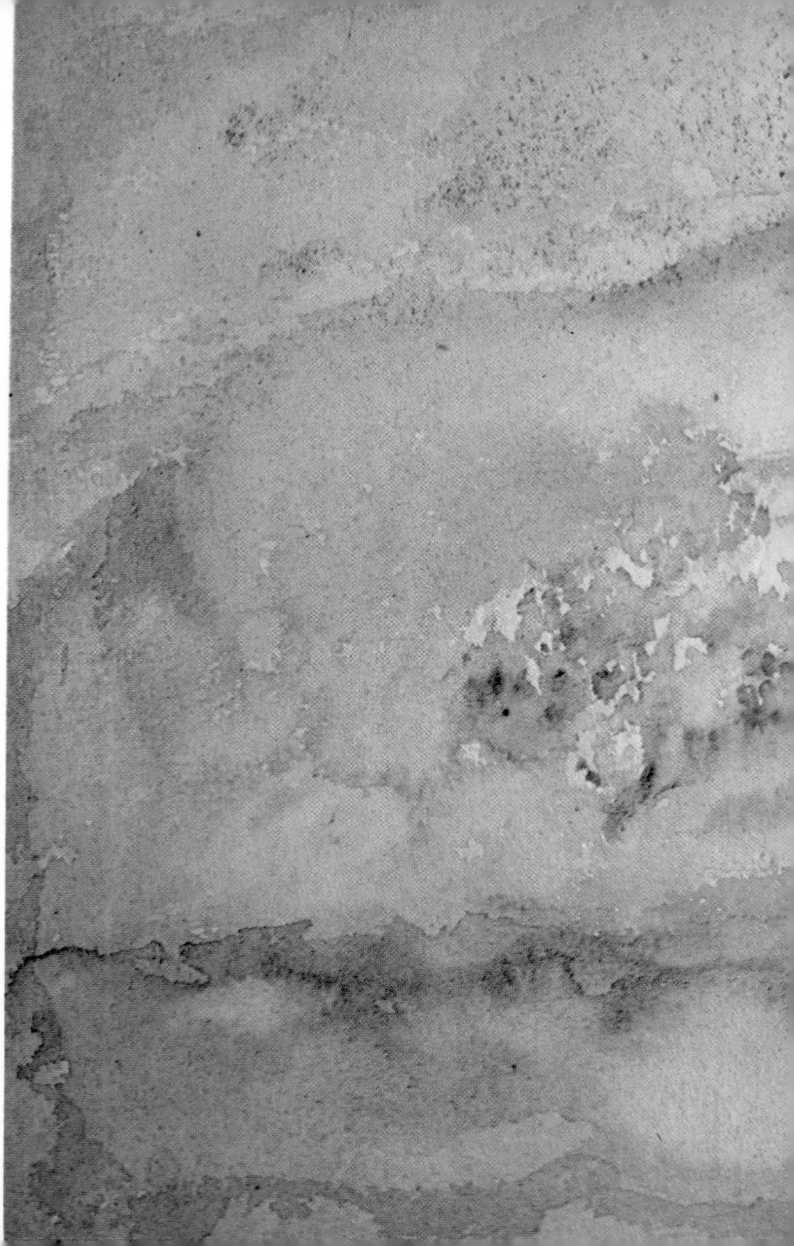

62 Little blond girl bathing 1887

63   Girl with a straw hat   1884

64
Two bathers
1896

65
Gabrielle and Jean (preliminary study)
c. 1894

66
Gabrielle and Jean
c. 1894

67
Gabrielle with jewels
1910

68
Gabrielle with a rose
1911

69 Bathers on a rock

70   Young bathers   1892-1893

71   Bather drying her leg   c. 1905

72   Blond bather

74   Standing bather   1896

75
Girl tying her hair
1892-1895

77   Coco writing   1903

78
Bathers
1918

79
Woman seated in the grass
1895

80
The Collettes' farm

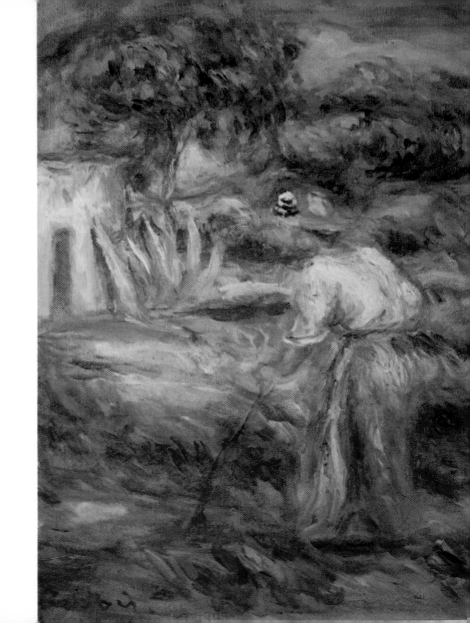

81
Bather lying by the sea
1890

82
Young girl in pink

84
Self-portrait
1910